Grade 1

Improve your theory!

Paul Harris

FABER *ff* MUSIC

© 2014 by Faber Music Ltd
Bloomsbury House
74–77 Great Russell Street
London
WC1B 3DA

Music setting by MacMusic
Cover and page design by Susan Clarke
Illustrations from Thinkstockhotos.co.uk
Audio tracks recorded and produced by Oliver Wedgwood, performed by Paul Harris
Printed in England by Caligraving Ltd

ISBN10: 0-571-53861-4
EAN13: 978-0-571-53861-4

To buy Faber Music publications or to find out about the full range of titles available
please contact your local music retailer or Faber Music sales enquiries:
Faber Music Ltd, Burnt Mill, Elizabeth Way, Harlow CM20 2HX
Tel: +44 (0) 1279 82 89 82   Fax: 44 (0) 1279 82 89 83
sales@fabermusic.com   fabermusicstore.com

Contents

🎧 Audio tracks for the Aural/listening activities are available to download from www.fabermusicstore.com/Improve-Your-Theory-Grade-1-0571538614.aspx

✓ Answer sheets are available to download from www.fabermusicstore.com/Improve-Your-Theory-Grade-1-0571538614.aspx

4

Stage 1

 Facts box

NAME	COUNTS	NOTES	RESTS
Semibreve (whole note)	4		
Minim (half note)	2		
Crotchet (quarter note)	1		
Quaver (eighth note)	½*		

* Two quavers fit into one crotchet count.

1 Write the correct name under each note.

_____   _____   _____

_____   _____   _____

2 Draw the correct note over each name.

Minim   Quaver   Semibreve   Crotchet   Whole note

3 Draw the correct rest over each name.

Crotchet   Quaver   Minim   Semibreve   Eighth note

4 Write the total number of counts under each of these.

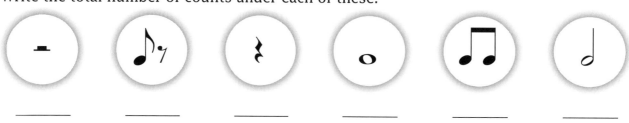

_____   _____   _____   _____   _____   _____

5 Let's do some musical maths! Work out the note-values to complete the sums in the balloons. Each crotchet is worth 1.

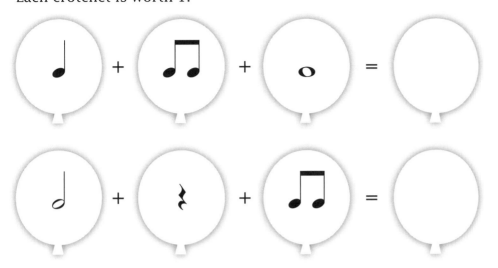

6 Have a look at this rhythm, then complete the puzzle questions below.

Theory isn't dreary

- Remembering that each crotchet is worth one count, what is the total number of counts made up from:

  – all of the ♩s? _____

  – all of the 𝅗𝅥s ? _____

  – all of the ♩s and ♫s combined? _____

7 All words have rhythm. Let's explore names:

Here's my name in notes:

Paul   Har-ris

Your turn:

 Theory box of fun

The word 'theory' comes from a very old Greek word meaning 'to look at things'. That's what theory is all about: looking at things and understanding them. Always ask yourself, 'Do I understand that?'

Making connections to your pieces

Look at any pieces you know and find examples of a semibreve, minim, crotchet and quaver, filling in the box below. Now find examples of semibreve, minim, crotchet and quaver rests. (The first one is an example.)

Name	Sign	Piece name and bar number
Crotchet (quarter note)	♩	Popcorn, bar 3

More connections

● Tap ♩s with your foot, then clap this rhythm.

Now try singing it to 'la' or your favourite sound. Can you sing the rhythm back to front?

● Get creative! Play this rhythm and improvise a melody using some notes from a piece you are learning.

Aural/listening

track 1

You'll hear a rhythm made up of groups of semibreves, minims, crotchets and quavers in turn. Put them in order of appearance by writing **1st**, **2nd**, **3rd** or **4th** in the boxes. You'll hear a crotchet beat first. So if minims are first, put '1st' next to ♩.

𝅝	
𝅗𝅥	
♩	
♪	

Stage 2

Time signatures: $\frac{2}{4}$ $\frac{3}{4}$ and $\frac{4}{4}$
Bars and bar-lines
The stave

Facts box

bar-line   bar

time signature   final bar-line

All time signatures are made up of two numbers:
- The top one tells you **how many beats** there are per bar.
- The bottom one tells you the **type of beat** you are counting. ⟶

Time signature code numbers

1 = o beat
2 = 𝅗𝅥 beat
4 = ♩ beat
8 = ♪ beat

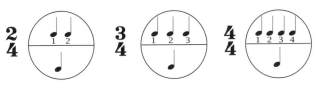

Time signatures with: 2 beats in a bar are in **duple time**
3 beats in a bar are in **triple time**
4 beats in a bar are in **quadruple time**

$\frac{4}{4}$ can also be written as **C**

---

1 Fill in the missing time signatures for these three rhythms. Choose from $\frac{2}{4}$ $\frac{3}{4}$ and $\frac{4}{4}$.

2 Fill in the missing bar-lines in these two-bar rhythms.

3 Add in the missing notes and rests to complete the bars.

(note)   (rest)   (note)   (rest)   (note)   (rest)

4 Work your way through this rhythm maze by selecting the correct time signature at the junctions. Colour in the correct arrows to show the journey.

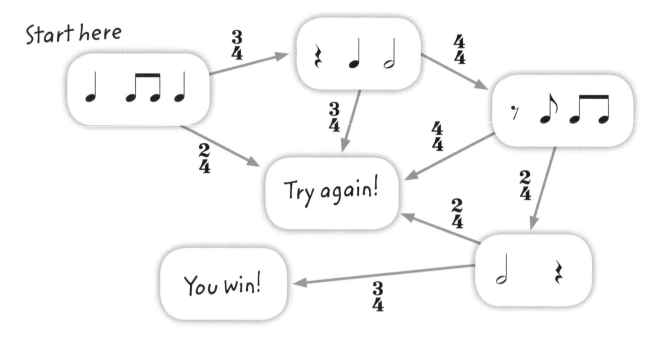

5 Have a look at this short piece and then answer the puzzle questions below.

Hucbald's one-legged dance

- How many bars are there in *Hucbald's one-legged dance*? _____
- The $\frac{4}{4}$ at the beginning is called a _____
- How many beats are there in each bar? _____
- What type of beat is used? _____
- Tap the pulse and clap the rhythm, then play the rhythm to your own tune, using notes from one of your favourite scales.

Theory box of fun

Hucbald the One-legged (who lived from about 840–930) was possibly the first musician to write music down. Here's an example of early music; play or sing what you think this might have sounded like.

Making connections to your pieces

Find a piece or song you are currently learning that is either in $\frac{2}{4}$ $\frac{3}{4}$ or $\frac{4}{4}$ and write out the first few bars on the staves below. Make sure you include all of the information and write clearly and accurately, with good spacing between notes.

Now try this quiz:

● What does the top number of the time signature mean? _____

● What does the bottom number mean? _____

● Are there any repeated rhythms? Write them out in the workspace below.

● Now write down any rests.

Workspace

More connections

● Using the same piece, tap the pulse with your foot and clap the rhythm. Alternatively, use 'home' percussion (saucepan lid and spoon, for example!)

● Play or sing the piece using the same note-values but changing all the pitches.

● Make up (improvise) your own short piece using the time signature. Give it a title.

tracks 2–5

Aural/listening

Listen to the four excerpts and decide whether the time signature is $\frac{2}{4}$ or $\frac{3}{4}$. Fill your answers in the boxes.

Excerpt 1	
Excerpt 2	
Excerpt 3	
Excerpt 4	

When you've finished all the work in Stage 2, sign **your** signature in the box:

Stage 3

 Facts box

- This is a semiquaver (sixteenth note) ♬

  ♬♬♬♬ fit in the time of a ♩:

  A rest that lasts for one ♬ is written as ⅞

- When two or more ♩ and ♬ are used
  in a row, they are **beamed** together.
  This makes rhythms easier to read
  by grouping notes into complete beats.

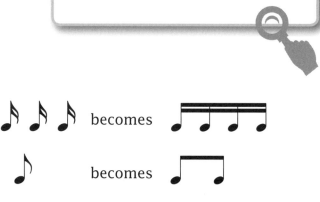

becomes

becomes

becomes

1 Rewrite this rhythm, grouping the quavers and semiquavers with beams and marking
the counts (beat numbers) underneath.

2 Add in the missing semiquavers to this $\frac{3}{4}$ rhythm.

3 Fill in the missing rests in this $\frac{2}{4}$ rhythm.

4 True or false?

♩. = 4 semiquavers **true / false**   𝅗𝅥 = 10 semiquavers **true / false**

♪ = 2 semiquavers **true / false**   𝅝 = 18 semiquavers **true / false**

5 Test your knowledge by completing this crossword.

ACROSS
2 A moment of silence
6 Found at the beginning of a piece *(4,9)*
7 Found in old houses or used to join notes together
8 The note with a hole in the middle. Has the same duration as 16 semiquavers.
9 What you might do when faced with playing too many semiquavers (two of these fit in a crotchet)

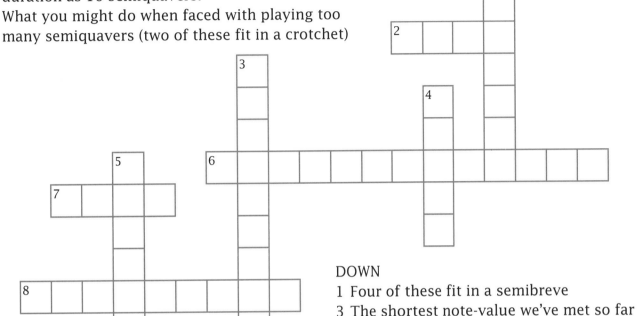

DOWN
1 Four of these fit in a semibreve
3 The shortest note-value we've met so far
4 A note that rhymes with linen (and can be split into two crotchets)
5 A line found at the end of a bar

6 Look carefully at this piece. Tap a pulse with your foot and clap the rhythm (or use home percussion). Then answer the questions below.

Hum-drum

● Put the correct time signature at the start of this piece.

● Crotchets (♩) and _____ (___) appear in every bar of *Hum-drum*.

● In which bars does this rhythmic pattern appear and how many times?

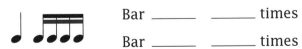 Bar _____ _____ times

Bar _____ _____ times

● Tap a pulse with your foot and clap the rhythm backwards – beginning at the end!

● Make up (improvise) your own four-bar rhythm, using the rhythm of the first two bars of *Hum-drum* and then creating a new rhythm for the next two bars.

Making connections to your pieces

Find a piece or song you are currently learning that is either in $\frac{2}{4}$ $\frac{3}{4}$ or $\frac{4}{4}$ (not the piece you chose last time!) and write out the first few bars on the staves below. Make sure you include all of the information and write clearly and accurately, with correct beaming for quavers and semiquavers.

Now take this quiz:

- What is the total number of bars in the piece? _____ How many bars have you written out? _____
- Do any of the bars have exactly the same rhythm? Write details here:

  _____

- Is the time signature: **duple**   **triple**   **quadruple**   *(circle)*
- What does the bottom (code) number of the time signature show? _____
- Choose a two-bar rhythm from your piece and write it below.
  Can you extend this by creating two more bars that answer the rhythm?

Workspace

More connections

- Tap the pulse with your foot and clap the note-values of your piece.
  Now play or sing the rhythm, changing all the pitches.

- Improvise your own short piece using the same time signature.
  Give it a title that reflects the character.

tracks
6–9

Aural/listening

Listen to the four extracts and circle the note-value that appears the most in each example.
You will be given a ♩ count.

Stage 4

Facts box

A **tie** joins notes of the same pitch to form a longer note (which adds up to the two note-values combined).

A **dot** placed after a note-head adds half as much again to the original note-value to form a longer note.

1 Join all the notes across the bar-lines with a tie, then clap and sing the new rhythms.

2 Join the notes with a tie and fill in the number of crotchet beats they add up to.

 = _____ beats

 = _____ beats

= _____ beats

= _____ beats

3 True or false?

= 4 beats   **true / false**

= 1 beat   **true / false**

= 5 beats   **true / false**

= 2 beats   **true / false**

=   **true / false**

=   **true / false**

Theory box of fun

Bar-lines are so called because they look like bars (an iron bar, for example). They were first used around the beginning of the 1600s.

4 Add a dot to complete the bars with the correct number of beats.

5 Transform this rhythm to reach the goal, clapping each rhythm as you go along.

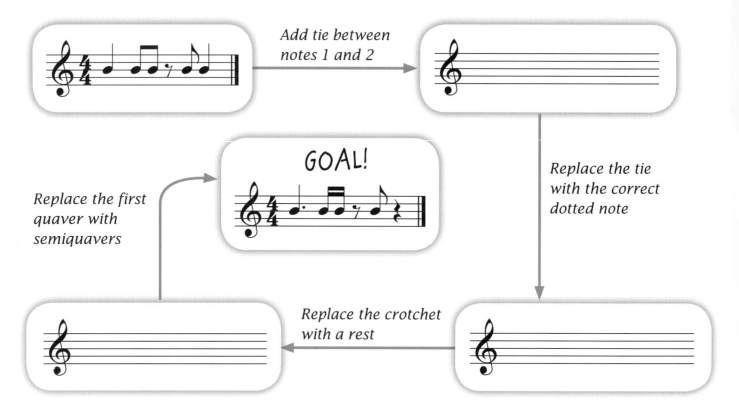

Add tie between notes 1 and 2

Replace the first quaver with semiquavers

GOAL!

Replace the tie with the correct dotted note

Replace the crotchet with a rest

6 Clap, play or sing these two rhythms, then take the quiz.

I'm all tied up

Beware of the dot

- How similar are these two rhythms?
  exactly the same   **slightly different**   **very different**   *(circle)*

- How many bars are there in each piece? _____

- What is the technical name for the two lines at the end of both pieces? _____

- In the second piece, what effect does the dot have on the fourth note in bar 1?

  _____

- Make up (improvise) a tune to either of these rhythms using the first three notes of your favourite scale or song.

Making connections to your pieces

Look through all the pieces you are currently learning and see if you can find
some passages that contain ties and dotted notes. Write them down on the
staves below, ensuring you include all of the information clearly and accurately.

- Choose one of the pieces that you found and, with a pencil, add in some more ties.
  Remember that a tie only connects together two notes of the same pitch.
- Try playing your piece with the extra ties; how does it compare to the original?
- Look again at the piece you chose. Can any of the tied notes that you added in be
  rewritten as single notes with dots? If so, write them down below.
- Now erase the ties you added in.

 Workspace

 # More connections

- Clap, play or sing the rhythm of your piece, then try doing it back-to-front!
- Create a musical bank using ingredients from your piece. Add them in the bubbles
  and then try improvising some music using them.

| time signature | key signature | dotted rhythm 1 | rhythm 2 | note 1 | note 2 | note 3 |

 # Aural/listening

Two of the following five pieces have ties or dotted notes (you can't be certain if they are written
as ties or dotted notes as they *sound* the same). Circle the pieces that *do* have ties or dotted notes.

piece 1   **piece 2**   **piece 3**   **piece 4**   **piece 5**

Stage 5

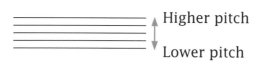

The word **pitch** is used to describe how high or low a note is. In music, notes are placed in different positions on a five-lined **stave** to show their pitch. Each pitch is given a letter name from A to G of the alphabet:

↕ Higher pitch / Lower pitch

A stave that has a **treble clef** shows a range of notes of higher pitches. The centre of the treble clef wraps around the second line of the stave (the G line).

A stave that has a **bass clef** shows a range of notes of lower pitches. The two dots are placed either side of the fourth line of the stave (the F line).

1 Fill in a semibreve on each line and in each space between those given.
Can you find the note G in the treble stave and F in the bass stave? Mark these with a *.

How many semibreves in total are there: on lines? _____ in spaces? _____

2 Trace over the treble clef and then draw four more. Make sure they all wrap around the second (G) line. Draw a box around the best one. Do the same for the bass clef, making sure the two dots are either side of the fourth line.

3 Draw four more semibreves on the G line on the treble-clef stave and four more semibreves on the F line on the bass-clef stave. Try to draw the notes the same size as in the examples.

4 Test your musical terms with this word search.

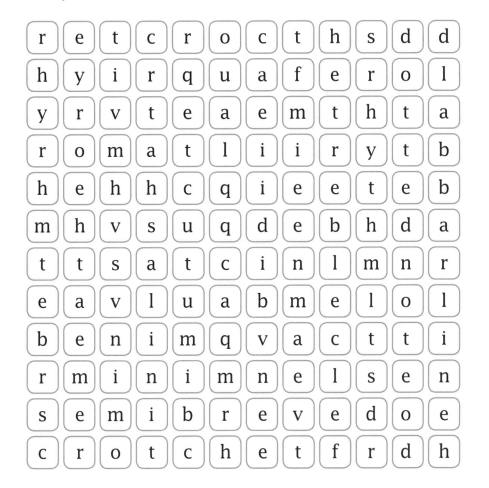

semiquaver

dotted note

treble clef

semibreve

crotchet

bass clef

hucbald

bar-line

quaver

theory

rhythm

minim

stave

tie

5 Have a look at this little piece and then answer the questions below.

Four bars ... **of chocolate please**

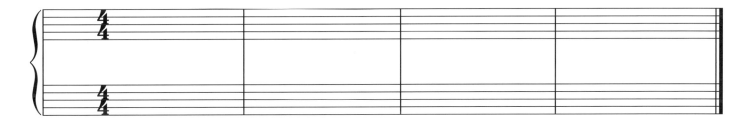

- How many lines make up each stave? _____
- How many spaces are there in each stave? _____
- Write a treble clef before the time signature on the top stave and a bass clef before the time signature on the bottom stave.
- Write a semibreve on a line in the first bar of the treble-clef stave.
- Write a semibreve in a space in the second bar of the bass-clef stave.
- Write any notes you like in the final two bars (but they must add up to the correct number of beats).

Making connections to your pieces

Find a piece or song you are currently learning and write out the first few bars
on the staves below. Make sure you include all of the information and write
clearly and accurately, taking particular care over your clefs.

Now try this quiz:

● Does your piece use: **treble clef**   **bass clef**   **both clefs**   *(circle)*

● How many times can you find:
(a) the note G in the treble clef *and/or* (b) the note F in the bass clef? _____

● Look at the bars you wrote out above. Can you write the note names under the notes?

More connections

● Sing the rhythm of your piece on either a G or an F.

● Write out the first few bars of your piece using the same rhythm, but with every note
written at a different pitch. Can you or your teacher play or sing it? How does it sound?

Aural/listening
track 15

High-pitched notes are usually written
on the treble clef and low-pitches notes
on the bass clef. Listen to these notes
and write down the name of the clef you
think they are probably written on.

1 _____

2 _____

3 _____

4 _____

5 _____

6 _____

Theory box of fun

● The symbol for the treble clef comes from
from the letter G, which curled around the
G line on the stave. Here's how it developed:

● Try drawing a treble clef in the air and then
find some clear space and walk a treble
clef! Now make up a piece or song that
suggests the _shape_ of a treble clef in sound.
Try this for the bass clef too, then design a
music bag with a treble clef on one side and
a bass clef on the other.

Stage 6

Facts box Where the treble and bass clef meet is the note called **Middle C**.

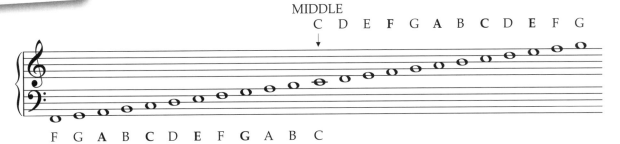

Let's start with the first letter in the alphabet – A.

- In the treble clef, A lives in the second space up. If we fill in the other notes that live in spaces we can spell **FACE**!

- In the bass clef A lives in the first space. **A**ll **C**ows **E**at **G**rass helps us remember the notes that live in the spaces of the bass-clef stave.

Note stems go up or down depending on the position of the note on the stave:

1 Here are the notes written over the lines of the treble-clef stave. Write out the notes again, this time in ♩s.

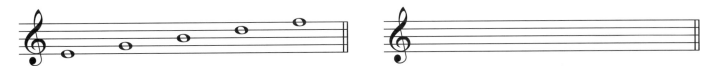

Make up your own words to help you remember them.

2 Here are the notes written over the lines of the bass-clef stave. Write them out again, this time alternating between ♩s and ♩s.

Make up your own words to help you remember them.

3 Name these notes.

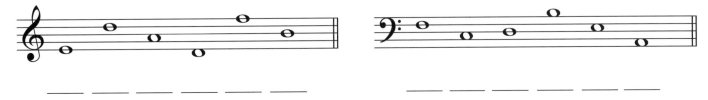

4 Name these notes to spell out the words.

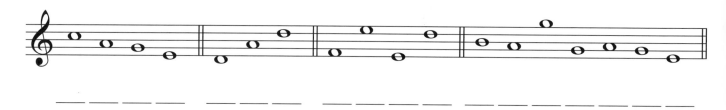

___ ___ ___   ___ ___ ___   ___ ___ ___   ___ ___ ___ ___ ___

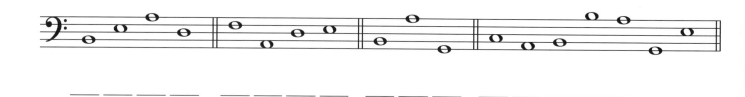

___ ___ ___   ___ ___ ___   ___ ___ ___   ___ ___ ___ ___ ___

5 Play or sing one or both lines of this little piece and then answer the quiz questions below.

Song of the humble bumble bee that sat on a little lettuce leaf

- True or false? In bars 1–4, both staves have the same melody. **true / false**

- What is the name of the highest note in the treble-clef stave? _____

- What is the name of the lowest note in the bass-clef stave? _____

- How many times is the note E played in the treble-clef stave _____?
  and the bass-clef stave _____?

Making connections to your pieces

Find a piece or song you are currently learning and write out the
first few bars on the staves below. Make sure you include all of
the information and write clearly and accurately.

Now try this quiz:

● Which clef (or clefs) does your chosen piece use? _____

● Can you find an example of every note name?
  Circle the letters of the notes that you find: **A**   **B**   **C**   **D**   **E**   **F**   **G**

● Which note appears most often? _____   Play or sing it.

● What is the name of the first and the last notes in the piece? _____ and _____
  Which of these sounds is higher? _____

More connections

● Sing a few bars of your piece to the letter names of the notes.

● Using the same notes, now sing or play them to a completely new rhythm.

● Ask your teacher or a friend to play from your hand-written score above.
  How accurately did they play? Ask them what they found easy and difficult
  about playing from your music, and then see if you need to make the music
  clearer for them to read.

Aural/listening

Listen to the three excerpts and write down
the name of the second note in each.

Excerpt 1 _____

Excerpt 2 _____

Excerpt 3 _____

Now write down the name of the third note
in each excerpt.

Excerpt 1 _____

Excerpt 2 _____

Excerpt 3 _____

Theory box of fun

The idea of calling musical notes with the
letter names of the alphabet was probably
first introduced by a French abbot who
had the wonderful name of Pseudo-Odo
of Cluny. He introduced this idea in about
the year 1000.

Stage 7

C major scale
Degrees of the scale
Tones and semitones

 Facts box

We often use words to help us measure things. We might use the words 'small', 'medium', and 'large' to measure our favourite drink. To measure the distance between sounds (or pitch), we use **tone** and **semitone**. The smallest distance is a semitone; two semitones make a tone. The word 'semi' means 'half' – like a semi-detached house or a semicircle.

- All major scales are made up of the same pattern of tones and semitones. Here are the note names and measurements of the C major scale:

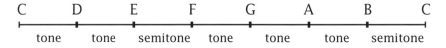

C		D		E		F		G		A		B		C
	tone		tone		semitone		tone		tone		tone		semitone	

- Every note in the scale is given a **degree**, from 1 (the lowest note) up to 8 (the highest note). For example, in C major, G is the fifth degree.

1 Label these examples as either a tone or a semitone.

___   ___   ___   ___   ___

2 Add the second note in each of these examples to create a tone or semitone.

tone   semitone   tone   semitone   semitone   tone

3 Number the degrees of the C major scale. The first one has been filled in for you.

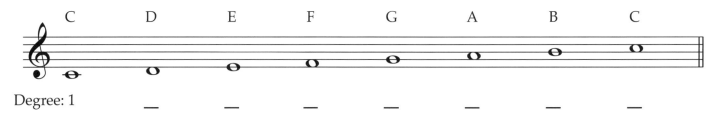

Degree: 1   __   __   __   __   __   __   __

4 Now mark the semitones of the scale above using a bracket (⌐⌐).

 Theory box of fun

The word 'scale' comes from the Latin word <u>scala</u>, meaning a ladder or a flight of stairs. How does a scale resemble a ladder or stairs?

5 Here's a musical journey for you. Start on the note C and then follow the instructions.

Instruction	New note
Go down a semitone	___
Go down a tone	___
Go down two more tones	___
Go down a semitone	___
Go up a semitone	___
Go up three tones	___
Go up a semitone	___

You have now reached your destination!

Which note is it? ___

Theory box of fun

The history of scales is <u>very</u> complicated! The first-known scales were invented by the Chinese around 3000 BC. Like ours, their scales were made up of eight notes, but each was related to a time of day!

So you had an early morning scale, a scale for lunch, a different one for tea, and so on! Can you relate the scales you know to a time of day?

Once you've filled in the note names, try playing or singing the pattern and then write it on the stave below. (You can change the title if you don't like this one!)

Tone right at the next corner ...

6 Play or sing this little piece and then try the quiz.

What goes up must come down

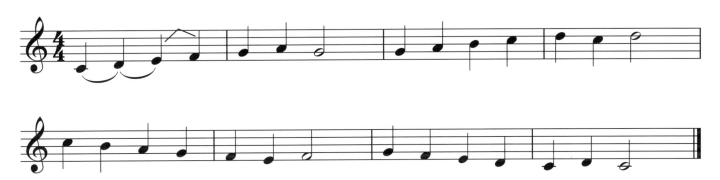

- Join up the notes that are a tone apart with this shape ⌣ beneath the notes and notes a semitone apart with this shape ⌃ above the notes.
  The first three are done for you.

- Now play or sing this piece, listening very carefully to the distance between the notes.
  Really try to notice the tones and the semitones.

Making connections to your pieces and scales

Find a piece or song that you're learning (or have learnt) in C major and write out the first few bars on the staves below. Make sure you include all of the information and write clearly and accurately.

Now try this quiz:

● Play the scale of C major and enjoy it! Think of the TTSTTTS pattern as you move from one note to the next.

● Look through the piece and circle any scale patterns that you can find. (Three- or four-note patterns count.)

● Choose one of the scale patterns you found and improvise a tune using these notes.

● Play and sing one of the tones that you found and listen to it very carefully. Do the same with a semitone and see if you can hear the difference (this will help you prepare for Aural/listening, below).

 ## More connections

● Looking at your piece again, choose one scale pattern and one repeated rhythm. Can you combine them to make a little tune? Try writing it down on the stave below.

● Now try playing your tune with some of the following ingredients: *forte*, *piano*, *staccato*, *legato*, *Andante*, *Allegro*.

track 18 ## Aural/listening

On track 18, you will hear some tones and some semitones. Listen to each example and write down whether it was a tone (T) or a semitone (S).

1 _____   4 _____

2 _____   5 _____

3 _____   6 _____

Theory box of fun

The word 'tone' comes from the Greek *tonos*, which originally meant a taut string that made a sound if you plucked it. A French word, *ton*, then evolved, which meant any musical sound. We still use the word 'tone' to mean the kind of sound we make. Do you play or sing with a good tone?

Stage 8

G and F major
Sharp and flat signs
Key signatures

Facts box

Sharp signs (♯) raise notes by a semitone.

Flat signs (♭) lower notes by a semitone.

- A **key signature** is the sharps or flats at the start of a piece that tell you the key. For example, G major is the key with one sharp. Any sharps and flats you might find during a piece are called **accidentals**.

- To make a major scale beginning on G fit the TTSTTTS pattern, we have to *sharpen* the F to raise it by a semitone, making it F♯, so the key signature is:

- To make a major scale beginning on F fit the TTSTTTS pattern, we have to *flatten* the B by a semitone, making it B♭, so the key signature is:

1 Draw sharp signs in front of all the Fs and flat signs in front of the Bs.

2 Write out the scale of G major using a key signature (the first note has been given). Now number the degrees of the scale and mark in the tones and semitones with a 'T' or an 'S' between the notes (it will be the usual pattern!)

3 Add in the missing notes and accidentals to complete the F major scale. Number the degrees of the scale and mark the tones 'T' and semitones 'S'.

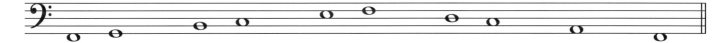

4 Write out the key signature and the first note for these keys.

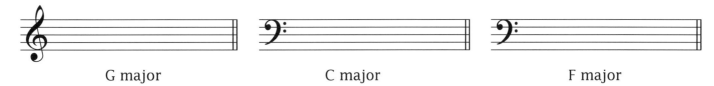

G major   C major   F major

5 Complete this crossword.

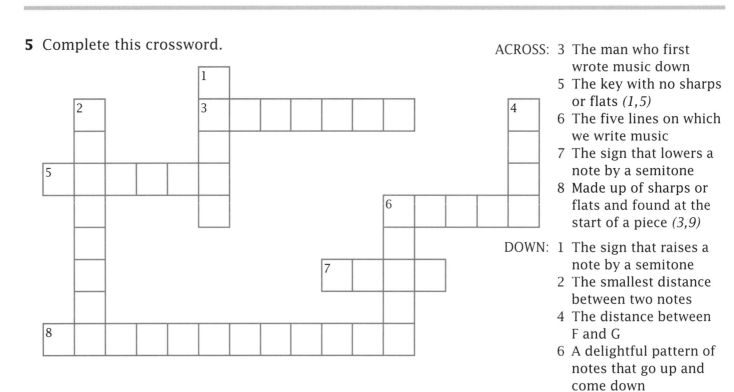

ACROSS: 3 The man who first
             wrote music down
          5 The key with no sharps
             or flats *(1,5)*
          6 The five lines on which
             we write music
          7 The sign that lowers a
             note by a semitone
          8 Made up of sharps or
             flats and found at the
             start of a piece *(3,9)*

DOWN: 1 The sign that raises a
             note by a semitone
          2 The smallest distance
             between two notes
          4 The distance between
             F and G
          6 A delightful pattern of
             notes that go up and
             come down

6 Play or sing these two pieces and then answer the quiz questions below.

Giant giraffes go gliding

Five famous fellows fidget fiendishly

● What are the keys of each piece? _____ and _____

● Circle the notes in each piece that are affected by the key signature.
  Which piece has more affected notes? _____

● Play the scales of F and G major. How do they differ? How are they the same?
  _____

● Name the degree of the scales for the notes marked * on the lines below the stave.

Making connections to your pieces

Find a piece you are learning or have learnt in G or F major and write out the first few bars on the staves below. Make sure you include all of the information and write clearly and accurately. Play it through and then answer the questions below.

- Circle all of the notes that are affected by the key signature.
- Can you find any scale patterns? They could be as short as just two or three notes. Write one or two out in the workspace.
- Find examples of semitones and circle them in the music.

Workspace

More connections

Play the scale of your piece (either G major or F major) and then improvise your own tune using the following ingredients:

- The notes of G major
- One of the scale patterns that you wrote down
- $\frac{4}{4}$ time signature
- Crotchets and quavers

Theory box of fun

The origin of the flat sign is very interesting. In very early music only one note, the note B, had a lower (or flat) version. Normal B was written using a square-shaped '♮'. The lower (or flatter) version was written in a more rounded way and has become our flat sign: ♭.

Aural/listening
track 19

Listen to these three extracts and match them up with the correct description.

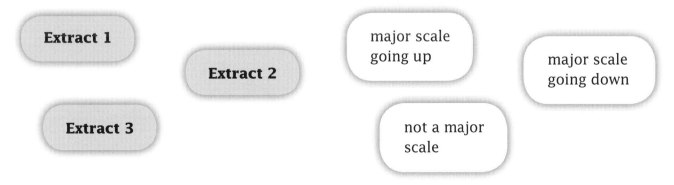

Stage 9

Facts box

The key of D major has two sharps: F♯ and C♯:

A key is made up of the notes of its scale. There's another pattern connected with each key. It's made up of three notes, so it is called a **triad** (like *tri*angle or *tri*cycle). A triad is made up of the first, third and fifth degrees of the scale. The first note in a scale is also called the **tonic** note. So, in D major, a **tonic triad** looks like this:

1   3   5

1 Write out the scale of D major and label the degrees. Remember to include the key signature.

Now circle the three notes from the scale that create the tonic triad.

2 Fill in the missing notes:

| 5th degree | 2nd degree | 3rd degree | 7th degree | 1st degree | 6th degree |
| of C major | of F major | of D major | of F major | of G major | of C major |

3 This scale has been written without a key signature. Add accidentals to the correct note(s) and then name the scale. Circle the notes that make up the tonic triad.

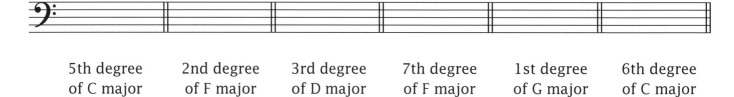

Scale _____

4 Name the key on which these patterns and triads are built.

_____   _____   _____   _____

5 Have a look (or play) through these two triangular pieces and answer the quiz questions.

I tried a triad while tricycling round a triangle

- Name the tonic triads in bars 1–4. The first one is done for you.
- Which is the only tonic triad not repeated in this piece? _____
- What are the notes in the tonic triad of D major? _____
- Make up (improvise) your own piece using the notes of one triad of your choice.

Triads and treacle

- Circle the notes in bars 1, 2, 3, 5, 6, 7 that form a tonic triad in the top stave.
- Now describe the key of each triad:

  Bar 1 _C major_   Bar 2 _____   Bar 3 _____

  Bar 5 _____   Bar 6 _____   Bar 7 _____

Making connections to your pieces

Find a piece you are learning that contains triad patterns. Write out a few bars that contain these patterns on the stave below. Make sure you include all of the information and write clearly and accurately.

Now play your piece through and answer these questions:

● How many different triads can you find? _____

● What is the full name of the tonic triad of your piece? _____

● Choose one triad from your piece and see how many different ways you can play it. Experiment with different rhythms, dynamics, articulation and the order of the notes.

Workspace

More connections

● Create a four-bar tune from the notes of the tonic triad and using some of the following ingredients. Write it in the workspace. Remember to add the key signature at the start.

Can you play or sing your tune? Give it a title that fits with the character of the music.

tracks 20–23 # Aural/listening

● Find the note C (from a piano or your instrument) and then sing it.

● Now sing the notes of the C major tonic triad. Sing the first note (C), hear the next note in your head (D), then sing the 3rd note (E), and so on:

Now sing the notes of the D, F and G major triads in the same way.

Stage 10

Facts box   An **interval** is the distance between two notes:

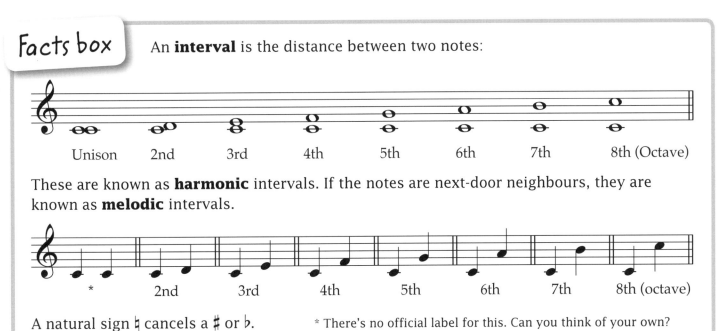

Unison	2nd	3rd	4th	5th	6th	7th	8th (Octave)

These are known as **harmonic** intervals. If the notes are next-door neighbours, they are known as **melodic** intervals.

	2nd	3rd	4th	5th	6th	7th	8th (octave)
*							

A natural sign ♮ cancels a ♯ or ♭.   * There's no official label for this. Can you think of your own?

1 Name these harmonic intervals.

_____   _____   _____   _____   _____

2 Name these melodic intervals.

_____   _____   _____   _____   _____

3 Write a note above each of these notes to make the interval described.

    3rd   4th   Octave   2nd   5th   6th

4 Add natural signs to cancel the previous accidentals.

5 Match up these well-known tunes with the interval that they contain at the start.
(If you don't know any of them, see if you can find a recording on the web.)

| Frère Jacques (2nd) | Oh when the saints (3rd) | Bridal March (4th) | Twinkle, twinkle, little star (5th) |

| My bonnie lies over the ocean (6th) | Bali Hai (7th) | Somewhere over the rainbow (8th or octave) |

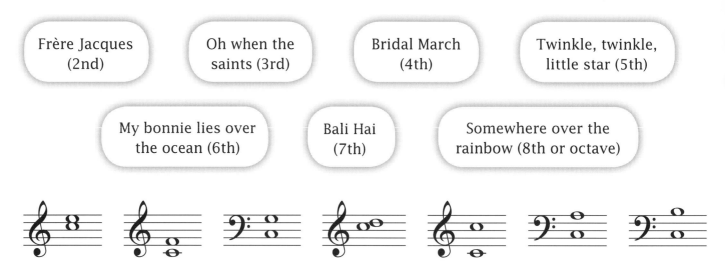

6 Play or sing either part (treble or bass) of this little tune and then answer the quiz questions.

Is it the interval already? Ice cream, please.

● In the treble-clef part, circle and label one example of each of the following melodic intervals:
   2nd   3rd   4th   5th   6th   7th   8th (or octave)

● In the bass-clef part, circle and label one example of each of the following melodic intervals:
   2nd   3rd   5th

● What's your favourite interval? Make up a piece that uses that interval as many times
as possible.

Making connections to your pieces

Choose a piece you are learning and then try to find an example of each interval you
know (they could be melodic or harmonic intervals). Write them out in the space below.

Now play your piece through and try this quiz:

● What is the key of your piece? _____

● Circle any natural signs you can find. Why are they there? _____

● What is the first melodic interval in your piece? _____   What is the last? _____

● Circle any of the following ingredients that you can find in your piece:

   a melodic triad   accidentals   a descending melodic interval   a harmonic interval

More connections

● Play the scale of your piece using some or all of these ingredients:

   ♩. ♪♩ ♩   *p*   *solemnly*

● Now play just the notes of the tonic triad in the same way.

● Finally, take some rhythms and dynamics from your piece and use them to play your scale.

Aural/listening

(track 24)

Listen to the melodic intervals on track 24 and work out which is which.
The first one has been done for you.

extract _____

extract _____

extract _____   8th (Octave)

extract _____   7th

extract _____   6th

extract _____   5th

extract _____ 1 ——→ 3rd   4th

extract _____   2nd

extract _____

Theory box of fun

The natural sign we use today developed originally from
the square ♮, which was used to return the flattened
note back to the higher one. Instead of the square ♮,
music printers began using a sign that looked like the
letter 'h', which eventually grew into our natural sign.

Stage 11

Facts box

Dynamics (range of loudness)
pp (*pianissimo*) = very soft
p (*piano*) = soft
f (*forte*) = loud
ff (*fortissimo*) = very loud
m (*mezzo*) = moderately
crescendo (or *cresc.*) = gradually get louder
=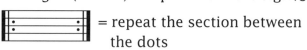

diminuendo (or *dim.*) *decrescendo* (or
decresc.) = gradually get softer =

Speed or tempo
Adagio = slow
Lento = slow
Andante = walking pace
Allegretto = fairly fast
Moderato = at a moderate pace
Allegro = fast
Accelerando (or *accel.*) = becoming
faster
Rallentando (or *rall.*)
Ritardanto (or *rit.*) = becoming
slower
a tempo = in time

Styles of playing or singing
Cantabile = like singing
Legato = smoothly
Leggiero (or *legg.*) = lightly
Staccato (or *stacc.*) = short or
detached =
> = accent the note

Structure
da capo (or D.C.) = repeat from the beginning
dal segno (or D.S.) = repeat from the sign 𝄋

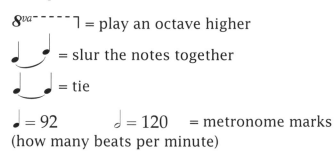 = repeat the section between
the dots

⌢ = pause on the note

8ᵛᵃ = play an octave higher

= slur the notes together

= tie

♩ = 92   𝅗𝅥 = 120   = metronome marks
(how many beats per minute)

---

1 Number these dynamic markings in order, from soft to loud (softest = 1).

  mf   *p*   *ff*   *mp*   *f*   *pp*

____   ____   ____   ____   ____   ____

2 Put these tempo directions in order of speed, from slow to fast (slowest = 1).

adagio   andante   allegro   lento   allegretto   moderato

____   ____   ____   ____   ____   ____

3 Name these performance markings.

♩ = 92   ⌢

_____   _____   _____   _____   _____   _____

4 Write these instructions as performance markings.

play an octave higher   **slur**   *crescendo*   *staccato*

____   ____   ____   ____

5 Can you find the 14 Italian musical terms hidden in this word search?
Write them out below and describe each one to a friend or teacher.

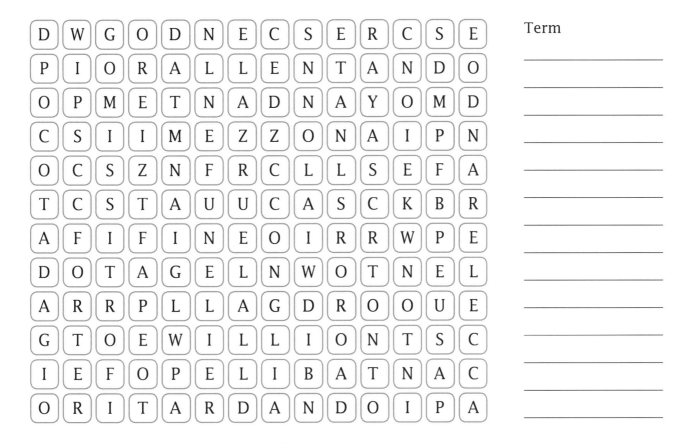

Term

_____

_____

_____

_____

_____

_____

_____

_____

_____

_____

_____

_____

6 Play or sing either part (or both lines if you're a pianist) of this little tune
and then complete the sentences below.

Waltz of the happy theory teachers

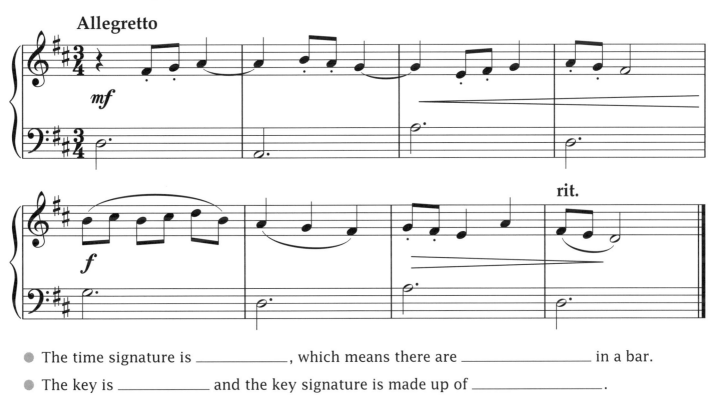

- The time signature is _____, which means there are _____ in a bar.
- The key is _____ and the key signature is made up of _____.
- The highest note (treble clef) is _____ and the lowest note (bass clef) is _____.
- The sign joining the A in bar 1 to the A in bar 2 is called a _____.

Making connections to your pieces

Choose a piece that you are learning that includes lots of different terms and signs. Write out the first few bars on the staves below, ensuring you include all of the information clearly and accurately.

- Write down all of the musical words and signs that are used in the workspace and then give their meanings.

- In the extract you have written out, replace or add the following types of ingredients:

  a tempo marking   a dynamic marking   a style of playing

  What terms and signs have you used? _____

- Now try playing this extract with the new ingredients and then with the original ones. How has the character and mood of the music changed? _____

Workspace

More connections

- Play the scale of your piece in the following ways:

  Piano   *Forte*   ◁▷   *Legato*   *Staccato*   **Andante**   **Allegro**

tracks 25–7

Aural/listening

Listen to the three excerpts on tracks 25–7 and match them up with the correct ingredients.

Excerpt 1

Excerpt 2

Excerpt 3

$\frac{3}{4}$, Allegretto, *cantabile*

$\frac{4}{4}$, rall., *pianissimo*

$\frac{2}{4}$, accel., *staccato*

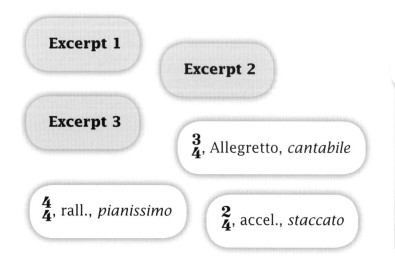

Theory box of fun

The first ever composer to use dynamic markings was the 16th-century Italian Giovanni Gabrielli. A 20th-century Rumanian composer, György Ligeti, used the markings *ffffffff* and *pppppppp* in some piano pieces!

Stage 12

1 Fill in the missing note or notes to complete these bars.

2 Fill in the missing bar-lines.

3 Write these scales using semibreves. Don't use a key signature but add all the necessary accidentals. Draw a circle around the 5th and 7th degrees of each scale.

F major, ascending

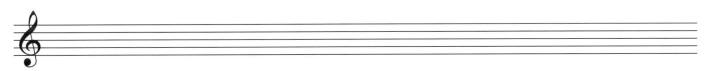

D major, descending

4 Write the key signature and tonic triad for these keys in both the treble and bass clef.

C major   **G major**   **F major**   **D major**

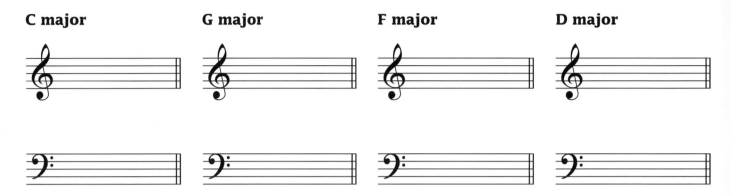

5 Name the degrees of the scale marked with a * and give the letter name of the notes.
The first answer is given.

6 Rewrite the music on the stave below using correct beaming, ties and dots;
then create a two-bar answering rhythm.

7 Next to each note, write a rest that has the same time value.
The first answer is given for you.

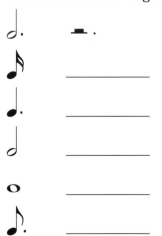

Theory box of fun

Triads also form the first three notes of another musical pattern — the arpeggio. The word arpeggio comes from the Italian 'arpeggiare', which means to play on a harp.

8 Have a look at this piece and then answer the quiz questions.

Take them sheep off my field

Traditional North West Buckinghamshire folk song

Explain the following terms and signs:

- Allegro _____
- ♩ = 120 _____
- *f* _____   *mf* _____
- *dim.* _____   *cresc.* _____
- > _____
- Dots over and under notes _____

Add the missing words in these sentences:

- The time signature is _____. It means _____ in a bar.

  Now insert the time signature at the correct place.

- The music begins in the key of _____.
- The music is written in the _____ clef.
- The tune in bar 1 reappears in bar _____.
- Give the letter names of the lowest _____ and highest _____ notes in the piece.
- Name a note that occurs but doesn't belong to the key of the music _____.

Circle one example of each of the following where they appear in the music:

- A semitone
- An ascending 6th
- An ascending 3rd
- A tone
- A descending 5th
- A descending 2nd
- A descending 4th

Circle the instruments you think would give an effective performance of this tune:

Violin   Organ   Tuba   Recorder   Triangle   Clarinet   Serpent

How many signs and symbols can you find in Theoryman?

Write them here

Congratulations

on completing
Improve your theory! Grade 1.
See you again for
Grade 2!